1963

is book

ALL THE PAINTINGS OF
MASACCIO

VOLUME SIX
in the
Complete Library of World Art

The Complete Library of World Art

ALL THE PAINTINGS

OF MASACCIO

Text by UGO PROCACCI

Translated by PAUL COLACICCHI

HAWTHORN BOOKS, INC.
Publishers · New York

Printed in Great Britain by
Jarrold & Sons Ltd, Norwich

CONTENTS

MASACCIO

Life and Work

"MASACCIO was born at Castel San Giovanni di Valdarno. He was most careless in external matters. He had his mind fixed on art and could by no means be induced to care for worldly things, such as his own personal interests, and still less for the affairs of others. He gave no thought to his clothing and did not collect debts owed him until he was actually in want. Because of this he was called not Tommaso (which was his name) but Masaccio (as we would say, 'Slovenly Tom'). He was so called without malice, simply because of his negligence, for he was always so friendly and so ready to oblige and be of service to others that a better or kinder man could not be imagined."

From this moving description by Vasari we can draw a lively picture of an unworldly artist who, having turned his mind to solving major problems in the expanding field of art, could think of nothing else and, as some documents confirm, seemed entirely oblivious of all that took place around him and in the outside world.

Masaccio was born on December 21, 1401, on the Feast Day of St Thomas, in Castel San Giovanni "on the hill" (the modern San Giovanni Valdarno), which was a large and prosperous village in the region of Florence. His father, Ser Giovanni was, at his birth, a very young notary aged twenty. His mother, Monna Iacopa, was even younger. She was the daughter of Martinozzo, an innkeeper of Barberino di

7

Mugello. Masaccio's paternal grandfather, Mone di Andreuccio, with whom the family lived, worked with his brother at making marriage chests, coffers and boxes of various kinds.

The family's name was not Guidi, as is still widely believed. This name was chosen by Masaccio's brother, Giovanni (called *lo Scheggia*), in his old age, during a period when most families of the lower and middle classes of Florence were choosing their own surnames. Guidi was a very common one, and may have been the surname of one of Giovanni's two wives.

At the end of the fourteenth century the Mone family was still lacking a full surname. Only at the beginning of the Quattrocento did its various members, including Masaccio and his brother Giovanni, begin to be described in official documents as *Cassai* (chest-makers) from the profession of their elders. But the surname *Cassai* was soon to vanish, as Giovanni relinquished it later in favor of Guidi, and the other members of the family died childless.

Mone and his brother lived, with their families, in their own house in the main street of the village. They also owned plots of land in the nearby countryside. Ser Giovanni died at an early age in 1406, and his widow, as was the habit of the time, was married again soon afterwards to a rich and elderly apothecary called Tedesco del Maestro Feo.

It is necessary to stress these details about the artist's family because some critics, having misunderstood ancient documents, claim that Masaccio's whole life was one of great poverty. For, if the artist did not experience poverty in his childhood in the homes of his father or stepfather, he was much more unlikely to have experienced it later when, as a famous painter, he was entrusted with many extremely important commissions.

Nothing is known about his early youth. The only information available proves that in 1422, when he was over twenty years old, Masaccio became a member of the Florentine Guild of Doctors and Apothecaries, which also included painters. But we can only speculate about his artistic beginnings (whether, for instance, he began to paint in Castello or went at an early age to Florence), for on this subject there is no information.

It has been stated that a fresco found in Montemarciano, near San Giovanni Valdarno, is by young Masaccio but there is no real evidence to support this view. It is more certain that his earliest known work is the *Madonna with Child, St Anne and Angels,* which was once in the Church of Sant'Ambrogio, in Florence, and is now in the Uffizi Gallery.

This work was clearly not painted by Masaccio alone; he was helped by Masolino da Panicale, whom Vasari states was his teacher and who, in fact, also helped Masaccio complete his last works, the frescos in the Brancacci Chapel. This seems to confirm Vasari's statement that the artist was helped by Masolino in his earliest known work but, as I will explain later, the young genius could not have received from the older painter, Masolino, anything more than mere technical instruction. Indeed, fascinated by the power of the new achievements in painting, Masolino's own convictions wavered and, from being the teacher, he ended by often imitating his pupil.

This view is now supported by the previously unknown fact that Masolino came from the same part of the country as Masaccio. It is therefore logical to assume that, as was the custom of the day, the boy was sent to the older master's workshop at a very early age. Certainly Masolino must have quickly become aware of his pupil's natural talent. This would explain the continuous collaboration—which lasted all Masaccio's life—between two painters of different generations and artistic inclinations. They had for one another that special regard which binds two men who share the same birthplace, especially when they have had to move from the quiet of their native village to the turmoil of a great city.

We do not know when the Sant'Ambrogio painting was completed. It could have been done at any time between 1418 and 1425. The picture shows a certain immaturity and, here and there, some concessions to Masolino's refined formulas, even in the parts that are surely by Masaccio's own hand. An example of this is the physical beauty of the young Madonna. The fact that Masaccio had not yet entirely renounced some of the traditional features of the art of his time could be explained by his extreme youth. It is probable that the painting was completed about 1420.

All critics agree today that Masaccio and Masolino worked together on this picture. Certainly four of the five Angels are Masolino's, the exception being the Angel in the top right-hand corner with the lively and deliberate movement of the left arm. Possibly Masolino painted part of St Anne as well, though this figure appears in very poor condition today, due to bad eighteenth-century restoration. But the concept of the central group of three figures in which, for the first time in art, space is realized in terms of perspective—as shown by the Saint's hand raised over the Child's head— can only be Masaccio's. In the florid Madonna, in the muscular Child whose head, brought into relief by the light, resembles sculpture rather than painting, there is an indication of the heroic quality and plastic beauty of the figures which, a few years later, were to grace the Church of the Carmine in Florence.

But even though one may fix the date of the Sant'Ambrogio picture at approximately 1420, very little is known of Masaccio's artistic activity at that time. In 1422 he joined the Guild of Doctors and Apothecaries; two years later, in 1424, he became a member of the Company of St Luke, which consisted exclusively of artists. Only in 1426 do we find documented evidence of a work by Masaccio. This, the great altarpiece for the Church of the Carmine in Pisa, is in fact the only one. It is possible that before that date he had painted, in the cloister of the Church of the Carmine in Florence, the famous fresco of the *Sagra*, commemorating the dedication of the church on April 19, 1422. Unfortunately, this work was demolished in the last years of the sixteenth century. For us, the loss is accentuated by the praise of fifteenth-century writers, including Vasari who records "a story marvelous by its artifice." There are also a few drawings by some sixteenth-century artists, including Michelangelo, which illustrate the crowds pausing to gaze in reverence and astonishment—as Vasari says—at the masterpieces in the Carmine.

On February 19, 1426, Ser Giuliano di Colino degli Scarsi, a notary of Pisa, commissioned from Masaccio a great altarpiece for his own chapel in the Carmine Church. The artist worked at this, with many interruptions, all that year and finished the painting on December 26.

Unfortunately this masterpiece, along with others, was not spared the injuries of time. It was removed from the church in the eighteenth century, dismantled and the separate panels dispersed. Only since the end of the last century was it possible to identify some of its components among the museums and private collections of Europe. This has made it possible to reconstruct at least the main lines of the Pisa altarpiece (see sketch on page 28).

To date, the following parts have been traced: the center panel, depicting the *Virgin and Child*, in London's National Gallery (plate 5); the predella, divided into five scenes (*Adoration of the Magi*, *Martyrdom of SS Peter and John*, *Legends of SS Julian and Nicholas*, plates 18, 19, 24, 25), and four small figures of Saints which probably graced the pilasters (plates 12, 13), in the Staatliche Museen, Berlin; the central arched panel, with the *Crucifixion* (plate 14), in the Gallerie Nazionale di Capodimonte, Naples; an arched panel with *St Andrew* in the Lanckoronski Collection, Vienna (plate 11); a second arched panel, with *St Paul*, in the Museo Nazionale, Pisa (plate 10). Missing are the two large side panels, depicting SS Peter, John the Baptist, Julian and Nicholas, and many of the "infinite number of figures, large and small" (Vasari) that appeared on the uppermost part of the great altarpiece.

The center panel, depicting the *Virgin and Child*, if compared with the Sant'Ambrogio *Madonna*, shows clearly the immense progress made by Masaccio in the intervening years. No concessions are made here to the past. The Madonna is no longer a florid young girl, but a middle-aged woman, holding on her lap her powerfully built Child, who is solemnly eating from a bunch of grapes held by his Mother. We are confronted here with the same grave majesty displayed in his great work in the Church of the Carmine in Florence.

Everything in this picture is subjected to the iron rule of relative distance. The Child's halo is shown in perspective, so as to detach his body from that of his Mother. Behind the compact mass of the two figures the throne, no longer indicated—as in the Sant'Ambrogio altarpiece—by a few essential touches, stands solidly built in space; its perspective is slightly foreshortened because the artist, when painting it, kept in mind the panel's height in the great framework of the altarpiece. In the forefront, the figures of the two Angels playing their lutes stand out in vivid relief, emphasized by the light. They give us a concrete awareness of the space between them and the throne, behind which, half hidden to increase our impression of distances, stand two more Angels.

In the predella scenes Masaccio was greatly assisted by his workshop apprentices. The two *Legends of SS Julian and Nicholas* are entirely the work of one of his helpers; in the *Martyrdom of SS Peter and John the Baptist* the master's hand is visible in the beautiful composition and in most of the small but powerful figures. But where Masaccio soared once again to really sublime heights was in the central scene, the *Adoration of the Magi*.

In the forefront, at left, the hut, seen in full perspective, set the stage for the sacred event, while the mountains in the background, defined in their essentials only, produce a clear and definite suggestion of distance. On this solemn stage the characters move majestically. Their bodies are strongly enhanced by the light coming from the left. (The page bending over to lay the royal crown on the ground is thought to have been painted by one of Masaccio's assistants.) Notably sculptural are the two male figures in the foreground; one of them, to increase the feeling of volume, arrogantly stands with hand on hip, under the cloak. Behind them, on the right, a group of horses are firmly held by the pages: we see here the ancestors of that glorious breed of horse that appear in the Renaissance paintings of Paolo Uccello and Piero della Francesca.

All the remaining panels show Masaccio's hand, even though the master seemed to commit himself rather less in the *St Paul* in Pisa, *St Andrew* in Vienna and the four small saints in Berlin. The *Crucifixion*, however, is probably the masterpiece, and one of the finest expressions of art of all time.

This scene was set very high up in the altarpiece, and was therefore given a foreshortened perspective. That is why the standing figures of the Virgin and St John shoot upwards and diminish in the upper portions and, in the kneeling Mary Magdalen, the long line of the back contrasts with the short legs. That is also why the crucified Christ, whose head, seen from below, is sunk in the broad shoulders, appears to be pushed backwards with his Cross. In fact, looking closely, one can see the lower part of the arms of the Cross left in shadow. This increases the whole effect of the backward slant.

The sense of space is thus vigorously achieved in spite of the golden background which itself tends to throw the figures forward, due to Masaccio's feeling for light and depth. To the immobility of the Savior, dead on his Cross, the artist opposes the frantic despair of Mary Magdalen, while at the sides, like blocks of human granite petrified by sorrow, stand the Mother and St John. The great tragedy has never since been represented with the same power of synthesis as in the Pisa panel.

After the Carmine altarpiece of Pisa historians are again silent. As a result, the most varied and contradictory hypotheses have been advanced with regard to Masaccio's greatest work, the decoration of the Brancacci Chapel in the Church of the Carmine in Florence. However, in spite of the lack of records, a careful study of the documents mentioning Masaccio and Masolino can lead to some fairly safe conclusions. In all probability—and contrary to what is commonly believed today—the fresco in Santa Maria Novella, with the *Holy Trinity* (plate 26), was completed

14

before the decoration of the Brancacci Chapel; the frescos in the upper section, later destroyed, were begun by Masolino without the help of Masaccio. This work was interrupted when the older master left for Hungary; the work was resumed, both artists working side by side, in or about August 1427. Masolino was then summoned to Rome, probably in the Pope's service, and Masaccio was left to work on his own on the lower part of the walls. But later he too had to go to Rome, and in such haste that he left one fresco unfinished (plates 68–9). He was to die there in the autumn of 1428, shortly before his twenty-seventh birthday.

The *Holy Trinity* of Santa Maria Novella must therefore have been painted before the Brancacci frescos. Vasari admired this work which, however, disappeared—hidden by an altar—when the church was reconstructed in the sixteenth century. It was not rediscovered until the last century, when it was moved from its original position and placed near the church entrance. Recent restoration, however, has brought out the fresco's original beauty previously blackened and over-painted, and the work has again been detached and replaced in its original position. Here it is now joined to the extremely fine lower section of the composition. This depicts a skeleton lying on a tomb—a section that, hidden by superstructure and lost during the first ten years of the sixteenth century, has now fortunately been uncovered.

Again in this fresco, Masaccio designed the perspective as seen by the viewer, and painted for an eye placed far below the level of the figures. This is especially noticeable in the figures of the Virgin and St John. In fact the artist, on this occasion, obviously decided to astound his contemporaries by showing them what could be achieved by using the new principles of perspective which were being formulated at the time. He had discussed these at length with Brunelleschi, creator of Renaissance architecture (the only man whose direct influence on Masaccio, as confirmed by the records of the period, is certain).

The *Holy Trinity* is composed within a great architectural frame, very suggestive, in fact, of Brunelleschi's style. In Vasari's words it is "a barrel-vaulted ceiling painted in perspective and divided into square compartments, with a rosette in each, so well done that the surface has all the appearance of being indented." The admiration expressed by Vasari echoes the astonishment which must have greeted Masaccio's bold innovations.

In such a frame the Crucifix is not, as in the Pisa panel now in Naples, the center of a great human tragedy, culminating in the death of a Redeemer who became man to save mankind. Violent passions no longer exist where Divinity has triumphed. Here we have the calm after the storm. An absolute stillness dominates the scene and includes the figures of the donor and his wife, kneeling at the sides, totally immersed in contemplation; the face of the dead Christ on the Cross shows great serenity.

In the summer of 1427, presumably, work was resumed in the Brancacci Chapel. As we have said, this time Masolino was not alone on the scaffolding, but was helped by Masaccio, whose reputation was by now firmly established. Theirs was no longer the usual relationship between master and pupil, but that occurring between friends, and possibly professional partners. Each painted on the lower part of the walls an equal number of scenes from the life of St Peter, to whom the chapel was to be dedicated. Working side by side with him, Masolino could not help being influenced by Masaccio. In his great fresco, *The Resurrection of Tabitha* (plate 81), Masolino—who probably asked his friend's help in tracing the architecture of the houses in the background and the perspective of the streets—tried to follow, as far as possible, Masaccio's example. He managed to imitate his former pupil's composition and outline of his figures, but was unable to reproduce the essence of his painting.

In the meantime Masaccio began to tackle the shorter side of the chapel, next to the great mullion window, where he painted the *Baptism of the Neophytes* (plate 34). But at this point, when the artist was perhaps reaching the summit of his art, and before we go on to examine, one by one, his various frescos, we should try to establish what was the secret of the innovation that made his name immortal and caused even his contemporaries to speak of him as the initiator and creator of modern painting.

Masaccio is universally recognized as the man who brought to painting a knowledge of the rules of perspective, thereby realizing space in which people and objects, proportionally depicted, find their correct place. The outer world, until then, had been expressed in purely symbolic and rudimentary terms. For Giotto, the problems of landscape and closer physical surroundings never existed. He had moved away from the absolutely abstract conception of the human figure in Byzantine painting and had succeeded in mastering that figure in all its human reality. But man, as conceived by Giotto, dominated an unreal world; and landscape, barely hinted at, was to remain extraneous to both material and logical reality. Masaccio now conquered space for this man, who had to live and move in the world created for him. His art marked the twilight of symbolic painting. After him all painting would reflect the reality of men and objects.

But Masaccio did not conquer space by use of perspective alone. He made use of light as well, and to a remarkable extent. Not light as applied without any rule by the painters of the fourteenth century, but a precisely defined luminous source. By illuminating from one side people and objects, and bringing out their form through contrast between light and shade, this luminous source creates between people and things, and indeed between their individual components, a sense of relative distance and thereby the illusion of third dimensional realization.

Having mastered the problem of representing physical surroundings, Masaccio began to shape human figures to occupy it. He already saw the human figure as something to be portrayed in all its monumental grandeur. He owed this concept to the only painter he could look upon as a master, Giotto. But Giotto's man, though perfectly conceived in the harmony of his proportions, retained the inaccessible majesty of that Divinity in whose image he had been created. Now let us look at mankind as depicted in the Carmine frescos: it is a mankind of heroes, although these heroes have their feet well on the ground; they are moved by tremendous will power; they know how to fight and are well equipped to do so. This heroic species will master the world created for it, but will not receive it as a gift. It will have to fight before it can dominate.

This is the special breed of men who populate the Carmine frescos. Their moral quality is unique.

The first scene, the *Baptism of the Neophytes*, is set against a severe landscape, limited in the distance by a mass of bare mountains. In the foreground the Saint administering the rites and the young man kneeling before him, are the focal point for organization of the movements and gestures of the whole cast. But it is the light which, shining as it does on the bodies of those who are waiting, creates in this fresco a great feeling of distance and depth. Vasari was especially moved

18

by the "naked youth, shivering with cold", seen standing on the right.

Masaccio's fame was made everlasting by *The Tribute Money* (plate 40–1), illustrating the passage from the Gospel of St Matthew (xvii, 24–27). When Christ and his Apostles were about to enter Capernaum "they that received tribute money" asked them for a tribute. Jesus then said to Peter: "Go thou to the sea, and cast an hook, and take up the fish that first cometh up; and when thou hast opened his mouth, thou shalt find a piece of money; that take, and give unto them, for me and thee." This part of the story is seen in the centre of the fresco. On the left, in the distance, Peter, "his face flushed with the effort", is taking the money from the fish's mouth. On the right, in the foreground, the Apostle hands the money over to the tribute collector.

This scene takes place against a vast landscape, limited, as usual, by a mass of mountains. On the left is a brief glimpse of the water in which Peter has caught his fish; a few tall, slender trees increase the feeling of distance but, so as not to lose the human figures in such an immensity of space, here on the right is the collector's house; its archway, drawn in perspective, contributes toward establishing the space of the foreground too, where the characters in the sacred event are grouped. The figure of Christ is the focal point of the whole scene. All around him, practically forming a circle, are the Apostles. They are stern and majestic, almost Roman in their gravity; their faith is unshakeable, their will indomitable. What a contrast they make to the tormented figure of the collector, seen from the back and rather harshly outlined.

The conclusion is shown on the right, where St Peter solemnly hands the money over to the collector. Here also there is a spiritual antithesis between the two, but the man who should be coarse and vulgar does not lack a certain dignity. For he too belongs to the Carmine's noble breed that Masaccio glorified forever in the *The Tribute Money*.

The last fresco painted by Masaccio on the upper section of the chapel walls was *The expulsion of Adam and Eve* (plate 51). It can be seen on the pilaster to the left of the entrance, opposite a similar fresco by Masolino, *Adam and Eve tempted by the Serpent*. Masaccio's fresco has become famous. Never has this tremendous drama in the history of man been more tragically presented. Even the heroes of the Carmine breed may be defeated—not by other men, nor by the forces of Nature—but by God. And when that happens their despair will be violent. Adam dares not show his face, but every part of him betrays his grief; the short arms, brought up to cover his eyes, the bent shoulders and the large head form a compact mass over the long, tormented lines of his body. Eve, being a woman does not need to conceal the anguish so clearly expressed in her distorted features but having suddenly become aware of her shame, mechanically moves her arms to cover her nakedness. Over the two hovers the avenging Angel, whom they do not see, but whose presence they seem to feel as they move helplessly towards their tragic destiny.

When he had finished his part of the upper section of the walls Masolino had to leave for Rome, and Masaccio continued decorating the lower part of the chapel. In the first fresco, a smaller one on one side of the great window, he painted *St Peter distributing the common goods and the punishment of Ananias* (plate 61), incidents recorded in the Acts of the Apostles.

The early Christians, who lived as a community under the guidance of the Apostles, pooled all their goods and each was then given what he needed. But Ananias, thinking it would go undiscovered, kept for himself part of the proceedings from the sale of a piece of land. Reproached by St Peter for his fraudulent act, he fell dead at the Apostle's feet.

The scene is set in the outskirts of a village, the houses of which frame both sides of the picture. In the center, and illuminated by sunlight, the sloping view of a tall building leads the eye towards a hilly countryside dominated, in the background, by Masaccio's familiar bare mountains. Far away, also flooded with light, a castle increases the feeling of distance. In the right foreground tower the figures of Peter and John, surrounded by their followers. At their feet lies the body of Ananias.

The mass of his fallen body, and the void above it, seem to restrain the peasants, led by a young woman with a muscular child in her arms. They wait for Peter to hand them their share of the goods. As in *The Tribute Money*, the contrast between the two groups is clear, for the stature of the two Apostles is monumentally expressed, and physically enhanced by the perspective handling, although the followers too have their own dignity.

On the other side of the window is a smaller scene, *St Peter healing the sick with his shadow* (plate 55). The Apostle, followed by St John and a few disciples, is walking along a street. The walls of the houses, seen at an angle, fill the left side of the picture, leaving only a limited space for the figures, which stand out vividly. The Saint advances solemnly, with head held high and brow creased in thought. Willed by a Divine power he seems unaware of what is happening around him. Grouped along the walls, waiting for a miracle, are the sick. There is nothing mean or miserable in their faces—they are stern and thoughtful. These are strong men, who can accept their misfortunes because they trust the power of their faith.

Once he had completed the two smaller frescos, Masaccio went on to decorate the great wall under *The Tribute Money*. This was to be his last painting, and he was never to finish it. It was completed about fifty years later by Filippino Lippi, when work on the chapel was finally resumed.

This large fresco includes two different episodes from the same story, *The resurrection of the son of the King of Antioch and St Peter enthroned* (plate 68–9). The son of King Theophilus, who has been dead fourteen years, is resurrected by St Peter through St Paul's intercession; after this miracle, Peter is seated by the King on a regal throne, and all come to honor him. The second part of the fresco, which is nearest to the fresco previously completed, is wholly by Masaccio, and possibly represents the summit of his art. The Saint is seen ecstatically praying as he sits on his high throne in a kind of niche carved out of the bare wall. Three men are kneeling in the foreground at the foot of the throne. On either side are groups of gentlemen and friars. The quality of space is exceptional and in this case, as in others, it is achieved by the use of light rather than by linear perspective. Some of the figures are enveloped in light, others remain in shade. As a result each form is more fully realized, while the distances between one group and another, and the components of the same group, become more perceptible. Perhaps by his handling of this composition which, because of its simplicity and lack of depth would seem to discourage all attempts at perspective, Masaccio proved better than he had ever done before the validity of his new methods.

The miracle is depicted on the left. This cannot be fully appreciated because the figures introduced by Filippino are mediocre when compared to Masaccio's characters, and as a result the "drama" becomes simple narrative. But here and there, where the master's brush completed certain parts

—in the figure of Peter resuscitating the boy, in the head of Paul kneeling in prayer, in some of the courtiers, in the seated King—the magic is still to be found.

In autumn 1428, Masaccio was urgently summoned to Rome where, with Masolino, he was to decorate the Chapel of Cardinal Branda da Castiglione in the Church of San Clemente. But actually he painted nothing in the Papal city. Florence waited in vain for his return and the completion of the Brancacci fresco. Instead, the sad news of his death reached them, and the grief of his friends was echoed in the words of Brunelleschi: "We have suffered a great loss."

BIOGRAPHICAL NOTES

1401, DECEMBER 21. Masaccio is born in Castel San Giovanni "on the hill" (the modern San Giovanni Valdarno), the son of Ser Giovanni di Mone Cassai and Monna Iacopa di Martinozzo.

1406. Death of Masaccio's father. Later, his mother marries Tedesco del Maestro Feo, an apothecary.

1406. Birth of Giovanni, Masaccio's brother, who is later nicknamed *Scheggia*. He too will become a painter.

1420 (*circa*). Possibly the year in which Masaccio painted the *Madonna with Child, St Anne and Angels*, for the Church of Sant' Ambrogio. This picture is now in the Uffizi Gallery.

1422, JANUARY 7 (1421 by the Florentine Calendar). Masaccio becomes a member of the Guild of Doctors and Apothecaries.

1422, OCTOBER 6. Payment of two lire by Masaccio to the Guild's steward.

1422–4 (*circa*). Possible date of the Consecration fresco for the Carmine cloister. This painting has been lost.

1424. Masaccio becomes a member of the Company of St Luke.

1426, FEBRUARY 19. Masaccio is commissioned by Ser Giuliano di Colino degli Scarsi da San Giusto, for the sum of eighty florins, to paint a great altarpiece for the chapel he donated to the Church of the Carmine in Pisa.

1426, FEBRUARY 20. Masaccio receives ten florins on account for the Carmine altarpiece.

1426, MARCH 23. Masaccio receives fifteen florins on account for the Carmine altarpiece.

1426, APRIL (*circa*). The brothers Tommaso and Giovanni report to the census of Castel San Giovanni that they are now resident in Florence.

1426, JULY 24 (1427 by the Pisa Calendar). Masaccio receives ten florins on account for the Carmine altarpiece.

1426, summer–early autumn (or first half of 1427). Probable time of execution of the *Holy Trinity* fresco in Santa Maria Novella, Florence.

1426, OCTOBER 15 (1427 by the Pisa Calendar). Masaccio receives twenty-five florins on account for the Carmine altarpiece. He promises not to undertake any other work until the altarpiece is completed.

1426, NOVEMBER 9 (1427 by the Pisa Calendar). Masaccio receives three lire on account for the Carmine altarpiece.

1426, DECEMBER 18 (1427 by the Pisa Calendar). Masaccio receives one florin on account for the Carmine altarpiece.

1426, DECEMBER 24 (1427 by the Pisa Calendar). Masaccio receives eight lire and five soldi on account for the Carmine altarpiece.

1426, DECEMBER 26 (1427 by the Pisa Calendar). Masaccio receives sixteen florins and fifteen soldi, the balance of the agreed payment of eighty florins for the Carmine altarpiece.

1427, JULY 29. Tommaso and Giovanni return a statement on their property to the Communal authorities.

1427, AUGUST–1428, autumn. Probable dates between which the frescos in the Brancacci Chapel in the Church of the Carmine, Florence, were painted, first by Masolino and Masaccio together, and later by Masaccio alone.

1428, summer or autumn. Masaccio dies in Rome shortly before his twenty-seventh birthday.

MASACCIO'S PAINTINGS

Color Plate I

MADONNA WITH CHILD, ST ANNE AND ANGELS, detail of central group (plate 1).

Plate 1

MADONNA WITH CHILD, ST ANNE AND ANGELS. *Panel, 175 × 103.* Florence, Uffizi Gallery.* Painted about 1420. Vasari mentioned it only in the second edition of his *Lives of the Artists* (1568), where he stated that the painting was in the Church of Sant'Ambrogio, whence it was moved to the Uffizi. Unfortunately the picture was irreparably damaged in a clumsy attempt to clean it, probably in the eighteenth century. The removal of repainting, during the course of recent restoration, has revealed the undamaged parts of the picture, and show clearly that Masaccio was helped, in this instance, by Masolino. Longhi was the first to establish what was painted by each artist, and his ruling has generally been accepted: four of the five Angels, except the one in the top right-hand corner, and the figure of St Anne, are attributed by Longhi to Masolino. Opinions differ, however, with regard to St Anne At the foot of the picture, on the platform supporting the throne, are written the first words of the "Hail Mary." (See also plates 2–4, and color plate I.)

Plate 2

MADONNA WITH CHILD, ST ANNE AND ANGELS, detail. Head of the Virgin.

Plate 3

MADONNA WITH CHILD, ST ANNE AND ANGELS, detail. The Child.

Plate 4

MADONNA WITH CHILD, ST ANNE AND ANGELS, detail. The Angel at the top right-hand corner, attributed to Masaccio.

THE PISA ALTARPIECE

In the fifteenth century Antonio Manetti, an erudite mathematician, stated that Masaccio had worked in Pisa. Vasari mentions in both editions of his *Lives* the great altarpiece in the Carmine Church of that city. This work was taken apart and dispersed in the eighteenth century.

As noted on page 12, eleven parts of the altarpiece have to date been found in various museums and private collections.

* All dimensions are given in centimeters.

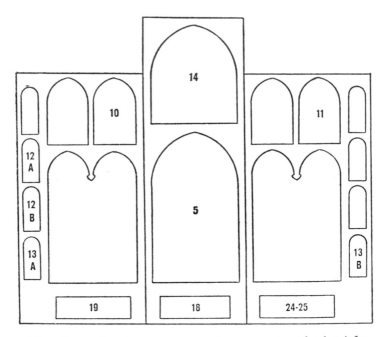

The above plan is a reconstruction of the Pisa altarpiece; the numbers indicate the corresponding plates showing the complete pictures, not the details. It should be remembered, however, that the altarpiece must have been about three feet taller than shown in our reconstruction. It is therefore very probable that along the top, where Vasari recalls many Saints around a Crucifix, there was a double row of panels. For the missing parts, see Lost Paintings.

Masaccio was commissioned to paint this work, on February 19, 1426, by a notary of Pisa, Ser Giuliano di Colino degli Scarsi da San Giusto. For the records of the various payments and other information, see Biographical Notes. The altarpiece was completed on December 26 of the same year, when Masaccio was paid the balance of the agreed sum of eighty florins.

Plate 5

VIRGIN AND CHILD. *Center panel, 135 × 73. London, National Gallery.* (See also plates 6–9.)

Plate 6

VIRGIN AND CHILD, detail. Head of the Madonna.

Plate 7

VIRGIN AND CHILD, detail. The Child.

Plate 8

VIRGIN AND CHILD, detail. Angel with lute (left side).

Plate 9

VIRGIN AND CHILD, detail. Angel with lute (right side).

Plate 10

ST PAUL. *Arched panel, 51 × 30. Pisa, Museo Nazionale.*

Plate 11

ST ANDREW. *Arched panel, 51 × 30. Vienna, Lanckoronski Collection.*

Plate 12

SS AUGUSTINE AND JEROME. *Panels, 38 × 12·5 each. Berlin, Staatliche Museen.*

Plate 13

TWO CARMELITE SAINTS. *Panels, 38 × 12·5 each. Berlin, Staatliche Museen.*

Plate 14

CRUCIFIXION. *Central arched panel, 77 × 64. Naples, Gallerie Nazionale di Capodimonte.* Recent careful restoration has revealed the painting in all its original chromatic splendor and the sculptural outlines of the figures are now clearly visible. Just above the Cross may be seen a Tree of Life that, prior to restoration was obscured by an ornamental scroll (painted at a later date) bearing the letters INRI. (See also plates 15–17 and color plate II.)

Plate 15

CRUCIFIXION, detail. Christ.

Plate 16

CRUCIFIXION, detail. The Virgin.

Color Plate II

CRUCIFIXION, detail. Mary Magdalen.

Plate 17

CRUCIFIXION, detail. St John.

Plate 18

ADORATION OF THE MAGI. *Panel, 21 × 61. Berlin, Staatliche Museen.* The two gentlemen standing in the foreground are believed to be Ser Giuliano, the donor of the altarpiece, and a relative. The page at right, seen in profile, could be Masaccio's brother, Giovanni, called *Scheggia.* (See also plates 20 and 21.)

Plate 19

MARTYRDOM OF SS PETER AND JOHN. *Panel, 21 × 61. Berlin, Staatliche Museen.* (See also plates 22 and 23.)

Plate 20

ADORATION OF THE MAGI, detail of the left side.

Plate 21

ADORATION OF THE MAGI, detail of the right side.

Plate 22

MARTYRDOM OF SS PETER AND JOHN, detail. The crucifixion of St Peter.

Plate 23

MARTYRDOM OF SS PETER AND JOHN, detail. The execution of St John.

Plate 24

LEGENDS OF SS JULIAN AND NICHOLAS. *Panel, 21 × 61. Berlin, Staatliche Museen.* These two scenes, generally acknowledged as painted by Masaccio's apprentices, are believed by some critics to be the work of Andrea di Giusto. In fact, the existing documents state that di Giusto worked in the artist's shop at the time of the painting of the altarpiece. The reproduction shows the left half of the picture: St Julian slaying his parents. (See also plate 25.)

Plate 25

LEGENDS OF SS JULIAN AND NICHOLAS, the right half. St Nicholas tosses three golden balls into the house of an impoverished nobleman.

Plate 26

HOLY TRINITY. *Fresco, 489 × 317. Florence, Church of Santa Maria Novella.* This masterpiece was probably painted in the summer or early autumn of 1426, or else during the first half of 1427. It is mentioned by both Albertini and Vasari, and was commissioned by Don Lorenzo Cardoni. He and his wife are depicted kneeling on either side of the central picture, which includes the Virgin and St John at the foot of the Cross. In 1570 a great stone altar was built in front of the fresco, surmounted by Vasari's *Madonna of the Rosary*. The *Holy Trinity* reappeared at the beginning of the second half of the nineteenth century, during the course of restoration carried out in the church. It was then moved from its original position to near the main entrance of the church, where it remained up to a few years ago. It was thought for some time that the fresco was in extremely poor condition; recent examinations, however, have shown that the surface had not been damaged but had been covered with other substances accumulated during nineteenth-century repairs. More than one old document stated that the image of Death could be seen at the foot of the fresco. Restoration carried out in consequence of these statements has enabled the fresco to be seen in its entirety; and it has been returned to its original site. (See also plates 27–33.)

Plate 27

HOLY TRINITY, central detail.

Plate 28

HOLY TRINITY, detail. The head of God.

Plate 29

HOLY TRINITY, detail. The head of Christ.

Plate 30

HOLY TRINITY, detail. The head of the Virgin.

Plate 31

HOLY TRINITY, detail. The head of St John.

Plate 32

HOLY TRINITY, detail. The donor's head.

Plate 33

HOLY TRINITY, detail. Head of the donor's wife.

THE BRANCACCI CHAPEL

The decoration of this chapel, in the Florentine Church of the Carmine, with stories from the life of St Peter is recorded by most chroniclers of the Quattrocento. It was ordered, Vasari tells us, by Antonio Brancacci, though some modern critics suggest that it was in fact commissioned by the latter's relative, Felice Brancacci. The vault and the upper section of the walls—which were destroyed during some repairs in 1748—had been painted by Masolino alone, perhaps in the first half of 1425. (He was still in the Carmine Church on July 8, doing some minor work for the Company of St Agnes.) After an unavoidable interruption, work was resumed, presumably in August 1427, when Masolino returned from Hungary. This time Masaccio was to help him. Together the artists painted the frescos in the central section of the walls. Then, after Masolino had left for Rome, Masaccio continued alone on the lower section. When he, in his turn, was summoned to the Papal city, he left his work unfinished. Some fifty years later the last frescos were completed by Filippino Lippi.

Towards the end of the seventeenth century the frescos were all but destroyed as a result of a reconstruction scheme planned for the whole chapel. That most of them were saved was due to Vittoria della Rovere, widow of Ferdinand II and mother of the Grand Duke of Tuscany, Cosimo III, to whom the Academicians of the Art of Draughtsmanship together with many others turned for help. Between 1746 and 1748, during the partial repairs, Masolino's frescos in the old vault and in the upper section were demolished and replaced by new decorations. A large rectangular window took the place of the old mullioned one, and a great marble altar was erected under the window. Since 1674 marble had already been used all along the foot of the walls and on the chapel's floor. Finally, the arch over the entrance—previously pointed—became semicircular.

During the night of January 28, 1771, fire raged in the church, but the chapel frescos were untouched. Only two pieces of plaster fell from the side nearest the sacristy. It must be assumed, however, that the pictures were considerably blackened by smoke. This, indeed, was recently confirmed when two protuberances had to be removed from either side of the marble altar. Small areas of painting appeared including the back of a male figure's neck in Masaccio's *Baptism of the Neophytes*, and part of another fresco by Masolino. The colors appeared to be much clearer than those of the other painted surfaces in the chapel.

In spite of Vasari's clear indications as to what was painted by Masolino and what by Masaccio in the Brancacci Chapel, criticism in following centuries created a certain amount of confusion, and the question was still being hotly debated during the eighteenth and early part of the nineteenth centuries. Today no one accepts the argument that Masaccio painted all the frescos in the chapel. Vasari's *Lives* once again has the final word.

Plates 34–81 show all the completed frescos and the most significant details of Masaccio's work in the chapel; the following plan shows the position of his single frescos— each number corresponding to a general view—and also those of

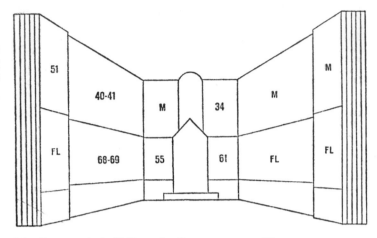

51

40-41

M

34

M

FL

68-69

55

61

FL

M

FL

Masolino, marked "M"—and of Filippino Lippi, marked "FL".

Plate 34

BAPTISM OF THE NEOPHYTES, *Fresco, 255 × 162*, showing the event as recounted in the Acts of the Apostles (ii, 41). It has been claimed that Peter's head and the portraits of the two men behind him were later repainted by Filippino Lippi. This, for technical reasons, seems impossible. In the author's view Peter's head, which does indeed show traces of repainting, and probably the two men as well, are by Masolino. (See also plates 35–39.)

Plate 35

BAPTISM OF THE NEOPHYTES, detail. Man being baptized.

Plate 36

BAPTISM OF THE NEOPHYTES, detail. Head of a neophyte.

Plate 37

BAPTISM OF THE NEOPHYTES, detail. Head of a neophyte.

Plate 38

BAPTISM OF THE NEOPHYTES, detail. Heads of three neophytes.

Plate 39

BAPTISM OF THE NEOPHYTES, detail. Heads of two neophytes.

Plate 40–41

THE TRIBUTE MONEY. *Fresco, 255 × 598*, depicting the episode, described on page 19, from St Matthew's Gospel (xvii, 24–27). Longhi believes that the head of Christ—less vividly drawn than the rest—was the work of Masolino. Lindberg claims that St Peter, seen on the left as he removes the money from the fish's mouth, is by Masaccio's assistant, Andrea del Giusto. In

St Thomas, the last figure on the right of the central group, Vasari recognizes Masaccio himself, while another critic, Salmi, insists that the same figure portrays the chapel's donor, Felice Brancacci. (See also plates 42–50 and color plate III.)

Plate 42

THE TRIBUTE MONEY, detail. The central group with Christ, the Apostles and the tribute collector.

Plate 43

THE TRIBUTE MONEY, detail. St Peter and other Apostles.

Plate 44

THE TRIBUTE MONEY, detail. Head of St Peter.

Plate 45

THE TRIBUTE MONEY, detail. Head of Christ.

Plate 46

THE TRIBUTE MONEY, detail. Head of an Apostle.

Plate 47

THE TRIBUTE MONEY, detail. Head of St Thomas, claimed by Vasari to be a self-portrait of Masaccio.

Plate 48

THE TRIBUTE MONEY, detail. St Peter takes the tribute money from the fish's mouth.

Color Plate III

THE TRIBUTE MONEY, detail. Head of St John.

Plate 49

THE TRIBUTE MONEY, detail. Head of the tribute collector.

Plate 50

THE TRIBUTE MONEY, detail. St Peter paying the tribute collector.

Plate 51

THE EXPULSION OF ADAM AND EVE. *Fresco, 208 × 88.* The leaves worn by Adam and Eve around their loins were added much later. (See also plates 52–54.)

Plate 52

THE EXPULSION OF ADAM AND EVE, detail. The Angel.

Plate 53

THE EXPULSION OF ADAM AND EVE, detail. Adam and Eve.

Plate 54

THE EXPULSION OF ADAM AND EVE, detail. Head of Eve.

Plate 55

ST PETER HEALING THE SICK WITH HIS SHADOW. *Fresco, 230 × 162,* depicting the story as told in the Acts of the Apostles (v, 12–16). Vasari believes the man wearing a toque to be Masolino. Probably the last man in the procession, with a white beard, is also a portrait from life. (See also plates 56–60.)

Plate 56

ST PETER HEALING THE SICK WITH HIS SHADOW, detail. One of the sick.

Plate 57

ST PETER HEALING THE SICK WITH HIS SHADOW, detail. Head of St Peter.

Plate 58

ST PETER HEALING THE SICK WITH HIS SHADOW, detail. Head of one of the sick.

Plate 59

ST PETER HEALING THE SICK WITH HIS SHADOW, detail. Head of a disciple, believed by Vasari to be Masolino.

Plate 60

ST PETER HEALING THE SICK WITH HIS SHADOW, detail. One of the houses.

Plate 61

ST PETER DISTRIBUTING THE COMMON GOODS AND THE PUNISHMENT OF ANANIAS. *Fresco, 230 × 162,* illustrating an episode from the Acts of the Apostles (iv, 32–7 and v, 1–6). See pages 20–21. The head seen in perspective behind St Peter's shoulders is probably a portrait from life. The facial features are too well defined for it to be otherwise. Salmi believes the last profile on the right to be that of Masaccio's brother, Giovanni, called *Scheggia*. (See also plates 62–67 and color plate IV.)

Plate 62

ST PETER DISTRIBUTING THE COMMON GOODS AND THE PUNISHMENT OF ANANIAS, detail. Head of a Christian.

Plate 63

ST PETER DISTRIBUTING THE COMMON GOODS AND THE PUNISHMENT OF ANANIAS, detail. Head of St Peter.

Plate 64

ST PETER DISTRIBUTING THE COMMON GOODS AND THE PUNISHMENT OF ANANIAS, detail. Castle in the background.

Color Plate IV

ST PETER DISTRIBUTING THE COMMON GOODS AND THE PUNISHMENT OF ANANIAS, detail. Woman with child.

Plate 65

ST PETER DISTRIBUTING THE COMMON GOODS AND THE PUNISHMENT OF ANANIAS, detail. Ananias lying dead.

Plate 66

ST PETER DISTRIBUTING THE COMMON GOODS AND THE PUNISHMENT OF ANANIAS, detail. Head of an old Christian woman.

Plate 67

ST PETER DISTRIBUTING THE COMMON GOODS AND THE PUNISHMENT OF ANANIAS, detail. Head of a follower.

Plate 68–69

RESURRECTION OF THE SON OF THE KING OF ANTIOCH AND ST PETER ENTHRONED. *Fresco, 230 × 598,* illustrating the episode related in Chapter 44 of the *Golden Legend,* entitled "De cathreda Sancti Petri." The part of the fresco showing St Peter enthroned is wholly the work of Masaccio. In the miracle scene, where Theophilus' son is restored to life, Filippino Lippi painted the group of five male figures on the left and the eight figures standing on the right, in addition to the lower part of the fresco, which includes the resurrected boy, the child next to him, the clothing of Masaccio's last figure, the body of St Paul and the raised hand of St Peter performing the miracle. The head of the courtier standing next to King Theophilus has been partly repainted.

Plate 70

RESURRECTION OF THE SON OF THE KING OF ANTIOCH AND ST PETER ENTHRONED, detail. Theophilus, King of Antioch.

Plate 71

RESURRECTION OF THE SON OF THE KING OF ANTIOCH AND ST PETER ENTHRONED, detail. Head of a courtier.

Plate 72

RESURRECTION OF THE SON OF THE KING OF ANTIOCH AND ST PETER ENTHRONED, detail. The heads of three spectators.

Plate 73

RESURRECTION OF THE SON OF THE KING OF ANTIOCH AND ST PETER ENTHRONED, detail. The heads of two spectators.

Plate 74

RESURRECTION OF THE SON OF THE KING OF ANTIOCH AND ST PETER ENTHRONED, detail. St Peter being worshipped by the faithful.

Plate 75

RESURRECTION OF THE SON OF THE KING OF ANTIOCH AND ST PETER ENTHRONED, detail. A Carmelite friar. (See also plate 76.)

Plate 76

RESURRECTION OF THE SON OF THE KING OF ANTIOCH AND ST PETER ENTHRONED, detail. Head of a Carmelite friar.

Plate 77

RESURRECTION OF THE SON OF THE KING OF ANTIOCH AND ST PETER ENTHRONED, detail. Head of St Peter.

Plate 78

RESURRECTION OF THE SON OF THE KING OF ANTIOCH AND ST PETER ENTHRONED, detail. Head of a Carmelite friar.

Plate 79

RESURRECTION OF THE SON OF THE KING OF ANTIOCH AND ST PETER ENTHRONED, detail. Head of a spectator, thought by Salmi to be a self-portrait of Masaccio.

Plate 80

RESURRECTION OF THE SON OF THE KING OF ANTIOCH AND ST PETER ENTHRONED, detail. The heads of two Carmelite friars.

Plate 81

HOUSES, from the fresco, *The Resurrection of Tabitha*, by Masolino. See Attributed Paintings.

Plate 82

Scenes from THE LIFE OF ST JULIAN. See Attributed Paintings.

Plate 83

CRUCIFIXION, in Church of San Clemente, Rome. See Attributed Paintings.

Plate 84

SS JEROME AND JOHN THE BAPTIST. See Attributed Paintings.

Plate 85

PORTRAIT OF A GENTLEMAN. See Attributed Paintings.

Plate 86

MADONNA WITH CHILD, SS JOHN THE BAPTIST AND MICHAEL. See Attributed Paintings.

Plate 87

MADONNA OF THE UMILTÀ. See Attributed Paintings.

Plate 88

REPAST FOR A CHILDBIRTH. See Attributed Paintings.

LOST PAINTINGS

*(This list refers only to the works recorded
by fifteenth-century writers and by Vasari.)*

THE PISA ALTARPIECE. Of the great altarpiece painted for Ser Giuliano di Colino, the following parts have not been traced: the two lateral panels showing SS Peter, John the Baptist, Julian and Nicholas, and many of those which Vasari described as an "infinite number of figures, large and small".

PROCESSION FOR THE CONSECRATION OF THE CHURCH. *Florence, Church of the Carmine*. This great fresco, considered by the above-mentioned sources to be one of Masaccio's masterpieces, recorded a solemn ceremony which took place on April 19, 1422. It was destroyed when a new cloister was built between March 1598 and September 1600. There are in existence some drawings by artists of the Cinquecento, including one by Michelangelo, showing groups of people from the great procession of eminent citizens and clergymen, passing before the church. Rather than actual copies, these are generally free interpretations of the original, and therefore can give us only a vague idea of the lost fresco. It has also been suggested that the five portraits of Florentine artists and citizens in a well-known panel in the Louvre, attributed to Paolo Uccello, are mostly, if not all, copied from the *Consecration*.

ST PAUL. *Florence, Church of the Carmine*. This fresco is also described by fifteenth-century writers and Vasari as one of Masaccio's masterpieces. It was lost in 1675, when a new chapel was erected in honor of St Andrea Corsini.

ST IVES. *Florence, The Badia*. When the church was rebuilt in 1625 the fresco was detached and moved to the convent. Since then nothing has been heard of it.

THE ANNUNCIATION. *Florence, San Niccolo*. It has been suggested that this panel is the same as a Masolino found in the Goldman Collection in New York, but the latter's iconography does not correspond at all to Vasari's description of Masaccio's panel.

ST PETER and ST PAUL (*Two Panels*) and REPAST FOR A CHILDBIRTH, "portraying a family". *Florence, Medici Palace*. These works are listed in the palace inventory drawn up at the death of Lorenzo il Magnifico in 1492.

CHRIST HEALS THE LUNATIC. This panel was in Florence in the care of Ridolfo del Ghirlandaio. There is a theory that it is one and the same as a panel attributed to Andrea del Giusto and now in the Johnson Collection, Philadelphia. In the author's view this theory is highly improbable.

NUDES. *Florence*. Left with Palla Rucellai. This was a panel showing two nudes, a man and a woman. Since Vasari's description of it, no other mention of the panel has been made.

PORTRAITS OF EMINENT FLORENTINE CITIZENS. *Florence*. Given to Simone Corsi. One of these—mentioned by Vasari—may be the *Portrait of a Gentleman*, attributed to Masaccio, and now in the Gardner Museum, Boston. (See plate 85.)

NATIVITY AND STORIES FROM THE LIVES OF SS JULIAN AND CATHERINE. *Florence, Church of Santa Maria Maggiore*. This was the predella of a triptych. In the second edition of his *Lives*, Vasari also attributed to Masaccio the main panels of the triptych. However, two of these are extant and they are clearly by Masolino. We accept the theory that a fragment of a predella—showing scenes from the life of St Julian, kept in the Horne Museum, Florence, and believed to have been painted in Masaccio's workshop—was part of the triptych.

FRESCO with no subject indication, perhaps a Last Judgment. *Florence, Convent degli Angioli*. It was mentioned in Albertini's guidebook (1510), and said to be located in the second cloister.

PAINTINGS ATTRIBUTED TO MASACCIO

(This list includes only those works which are still being discussed by modern critics.)

Plate 81

THE RESURRECTION OF TABITHA. *Florence, Church of the Carmine, Brancacci Chapel.* No one accepts this attribution today. Some critics, however, recognize Masaccio's hand in the painting of the crippled man. Recently Longhi, reviving a previous theory by Gamba, suggested that Masaccio may have painted for his old master the architectural background in the Piazza and the tiny figures seen moving in the distance. Masaccio may have outlined the perspective of the streets and the architecture of the houses leaving Masolino to enrich the picture with his analytical depictions of people, animals and objects seen near the windows. Perhaps Masaccio may have painted, among the little figures in the Piazza, the two characters sitting on a low wall in front of a house and, to the right of them, the man behind the disciple following St Peter.

Plate 82

Scenes from THE LIFE OF ST JULIAN. *Florence, Horne Museum. Fragment of a predella, panel, 24 × 43.* This painting, which unfortunately is in extremely poor condition, was attributed with some doubt to Masaccio by Gamba, and is generally accepted as the work of the master or of his workshop. The author believes it to be undoubtedly by Masaccio and has not previously discussed this painting, not so much because of the controversy still centered around its origin, but because of its present poor state. Indeed, the abrasions on the painted surface are such that the panel can only be appreciated by those patient enough to discover for themselves the traces of its former beauty. Gamba was probably right, too, in assuming that this fragment was part of the lost triptych of Santa Maria Maggiore. (See Lost Paintings.) Two of the main panels of the triptych, identified in recent decades, are certainly by Masolino, but it must be remembered that Vasari, in the first edition of his *Lives*, wrote that only the predella had been painted by Masaccio. The theory has also been submitted—but not very convincingly—that the panel may have been a kind of first draft of that part of the Pisa altarpiece dealing with the same subject. The painting has furthermore been described as an early work of Domenico Veneziano and has also been attributed to Pesello, an artist mentioned in many documents, although none of his pictures have been identified to date.

Plate 83

CRUCIFIXION AND STORIES OF SS CATHERINE AND AMBROSE. *Rome, Church of San Clemente, the Branda da Castiglione Chapel.* It was Vasari who first attributed these frescos to Masaccio, but some nineteenth-century critics disagreed with him. Those modern critics who still believe that Masaccio contributed to these frescos feel, however, that he only painted the great Crucifixion and possibly only some parts of that. It is the author's contention that this fresco, which dates back to 1428, cannot be considered the work of Masaccio. Alongside the work of Masolino may be seen—quite clearly—the hand of another noteworthy and hitherto unknown master. This artist, while displaying both understanding and style of the

great Florentine painter, reveals none the less a style of his own—one that is to some extent still linked to that of the past. Brandi has recently suggested—basing his hypothesis too on the equally fine outline discovered when the fresco was detached from the wall—that this unknown artist might possibly be identified as Domenico Veneziano.

Plate 84

SS JEROME AND JOHN THE BAPTIST. *London, National Gallery. Panel, 114 × 55.* Attributed by Sir Kenneth Clark. Originally this was a single panel painted on both sides, which was part of a triptych in Rome's Santa Maria Maggiore, combining a St Liberius and a St Matthias by Masolino. The second edition of Vasari's *Lives* attributed it to Masaccio, but the remaining panels, kept in Naples and Philadelphia, are now almost universally recognized as the work of Masolino or one of his assistants. At first the author was reluctant to believe—with Sir Kenneth—that the triptych was begun in 1425 by Masaccio alone, who painted the London panel and a few parts of the other two, and completed by Masolino in 1428. On the other hand, existing documents and other arguments would discourage the thesis that the whole work was executed in 1425. Finally, proofs both historical and stylistic, seem to contradict the supposition that the panel was painted in the first half of 1424 or previously; in other words, painted in the only period when a joint journey to Rome by the two artists—for reasons other than the San Clemente decorations—would seem possible. One felt inclined to assume, therefore, that the whole triptych was begun and finished in 1428, and that the two artists started

39

working at it together, the senior painter choosing for himself the central and more important part, and Masaccio contributing to the essentials, such as the positioning of the figures and faces, and to some details (including without doubt John the Baptist's foot). But his work was interrupted by death and completed by Masolino, who less weakened its heroic fibre. A closer study of the whole problem has compelled the author to modify his conclusions to some extent, which were based on the premiss that the work could not have been executed before 1428. It is practically impossible to believe Masaccio's powers could have so greatly declined so soon after the painting of the Carmine frescos. Indeed, for this very reason, Sir Kenneth cannot believe that the panel was painted prior to the Brancacci Chapel decorations.

Plate 85

PORTRAIT OF A GENTLEMAN. *Boston, Gardner Museum. Panel.* This was first attributed to Masaccio by Berenson, and most critics agree: the iconography recalls vividly that of the two male figures in the Carmine fresco, the *Baptism of the Neophytes*.

Plate 86

MADONNA WITH CHILD, SS JOHN THE BAPTIST AND MICHAEL. *Montemarciano, Church of the Madonna delle Grazie, the Oratory.* The first to attribute this fresco to Masaccio was Magherini-Graziani. Many critics believe it to be one of the master's early efforts, painted in his native village before he moved to Florence. Others see in this picture a similarity to the style of Francesco d'Antonio.

Plate 87

MADONNA OF THE UMILTÀ. *Washington, National Gallery of Art.*

The panel was first attributed to Masaccio by Berenson who, however, omitted it from the last edition of his lists. Almost all the critics agree, but the very poor condition of the picture makes any definite verdict impossible. The entire surface has been repainted and only when the repaints are removed will a clear judgement be possible. However, the basic style of the composition would hardly appear to be that of Masaccio.

Plate 88

REPAST FOR A CHILDBIRTH. *Berlin, Staatliche Museen. Panel.* Attributed to Masaccio as far back as the nineteenth century, when it was part of a private collection. Most critics still agree, although other artists have been suggested, including Andrea del Giusto and Domenico di Bartolo, an artist from Siena. The author believes this work to have been painted in the fourth decade of the fifteenth century, that is, after Masaccio's death.

ST PETER PREACHING TO THE MADMEN. *Florence, Church of the Carmine, Brancacci Chapel.* Practically all critics have now rejected the attribution of this fresco, judging it to be by Masolino. More recently Longhi has submitted the theory that Masaccio may have painted the figure of Peter (but not his head) and the three young men behind him.

ST PAUL VISITING ST PETER IN PRISON. *Florence, Church of the Carmine, Brancacci Chapel.* Some believe that this fresco by Filippino Lippi was begun, or at least drawn, by Masaccio; this would be especially true of part of St Paul's figure. One might suggest that Masaccio had traced an outline of the composition on the unplastered wall, and that Lippi, for what it was worth, might have used this outline for his picture.

PORTRAIT OF A GENTLEMAN. *Washington, National Gallery of Art (Mellon Collection).* The attribution dates back to the nineteenth century and was recently revived by Salmi.

THE REDEEMER RESURRECTED. *Strasbourg, Musée des Beaux-Arts.* This panel was attributed to Masaccio, not without doubts and certainly as an early work, first by Berenson and then by Giglioli. Others believe it to be by Francesco d'Antonio.

THE ETERNAL FATHER. *London, National Gallery. Panel.* This attribution, by Philipps, was accepted by Giglioli, Lindberg and Berenson, who saw it as part of the Pisa altarpiece. Most critics, however, think it the work of Masaccio's assistants or of an imitator. Some believe it to be a Venetian painting, recalling the early period of Giovanni Bellini.

MADONNA WITH CHILD. *Rome.* Attributed to Masaccio by Longhi.

This picture was recently shown in the Palazzo Venezia, together with other masterpieces recovered from Germany.

HOLY FAMILY. *Altenburg, Lindenau Museum.* Longhi, who had first ascribed this painting "directly to Masaccio", later called it "worthy of Masaccio's early period." Attributed by others to Ansuino da Forlì, to Filippo Lippi, to an anonymous painter from Padua influenced by Lippi, and to Domenico Morone.

PORTRAIT OF A GENTLEMAN. *Chambery, Musée Benoît Molin.* Doubtfully attributed to Masaccio by Berenson. Others, with varying degrees of certainty, believe it to be by Paolo Uccello.

TWO PORTRAITS OF GENTLEMEN. *Zürich, Landolthaus. Panels.* Berenson thought them to be copies of lost originals by Masaccio. Other experts attribute them to Andrea del Castagno, Paolo Uccello, Domenico Veneziano and Petrus Christus.

LOCATION OF PAINTINGS

ALTENBURG

LINDENAU MUSEUM

Holy Family (attribution).

BERLIN

STAATLICHE MUSEEN

Sections of the altarpiece from the Church of the Carmine, Pisa:
SS Augustine and Jerome (plate 12);
Two Carmelite saints (plate 13);
Adoration of the Magi (plates 18, 20, 21);
Martyrdom of SS Peter and John (plates 19, 22, 23);
Legends of SS Julian and Nicholas (plates 24, 25; from the artist's workshop);
Repast for a childbirth (plate 88; attribution).

BOSTON

GARDNER MUSEUM

Portrait of a gentleman (plate 85; attribution).

CHAMBERY

MUSÉE BENOIT MOLIN

Portrait of a gentleman (attribution)

FLORENCE

UFFIZI GALLERY

Madonna with Child, St Anne and Angels (plates 1, 2, 3, 4 and color plate I).

CHURCH OF SANTA MARIA NOVELLA

Holy Trinity (plates 26, 27, 28, 29, 30, 31, 32, 33).

CHURCH OF THE CARMINE, BRANCACCI CHAPEL

Baptism of the Neophytes (plates 34, 35, 36, 37, 38, 39).
The Tribute Money (plates 40–41, 42, 43, 44, 45, 46, 47, 48, 49, 50 and color plate III).
The expulsion of Adam and Eve (plates 51, 52, 53, 54).
St Peter healing the sick with his shadow (plates 55, 56, 57, 58, 59, 60).
St Peter distributing the common goods and the punishment of Ananias (plates 61, 62, 63, 64, 65, 66, 67 and color plate IV).
The resurrection of the son of the King of Antioch and St Peter enthroned (plates 68–69, 70, 71, 72, 73, 74, 75, 76, 77, 78, 79, 80: the fresco completed by Filippino Lippi).
Houses, from the fresco, *The Resurrection of Tabitha* by Masolino (plate 81; attribution).
St Peter preaching to the madmen (attribution).
St Paul visiting St Peter in prison (attribution).

HORNE MUSEUM

Scenes from *The life of St Julian* (plate 82; attribution).

LONDON

NATIONAL GALLERY

Virgin and Child, center panel of the altarpiece from the Church of the Carmine, Pisa (plates 5, 6, 7, 8, 9).
The Eternal Father (attribution).
SS Jerome and John the Baptist (plate 84; attribution)

MONTEMARCIANO

CHURCH OF THE MADONNA DELLE GRAZIE, THE ORATORY

Madonna with Child, SS John the Baptist and Michael (plate 86; attribution).

NAPLES

GALLERIE NAZIONALE DI CAPODIMONTE

Crucifixion, central arched panel of the altarpiece from the Church of the Carmine, Pisa (plates 14, 15, 16, 17 and color plate II).

PISA

MUSEO NAZIONALE

St Paul, arched panel of the altarpiece from the Church of the Carmine, Pisa (plate 10).

ROME

CHURCH OF SAN CLEMENTE

Crucifixion and stories of SS Catherine and Ambrose (plate 83; attribution).

RECENTLY SHOWN IN THE PALAZZO VENEZIA WITH OTHER MASTERPIECES RECOVERED FROM GERMANY

Madonna with Child (attribution).

STRASBOURG

MUSÉE DES BEAUX-ARTS

The Redeemer Resurrected (attribution).

VIENNA

LANCKORONSKI COLLECTION

St Andrew, arched panel of the altarpiece from the Church of the Carmine, Pisa (plate 11).

WASHINGTON

NATIONAL GALLERY OF ART

Madonna of the Umiltà (plate 87; attribution).
Portrait of a gentleman (attribution).

ZÜRICH

LANDOLTHAUS

Two portraits of gentlemen (copies).

SELECTED CRITICISM

He was an excellent imitator of Nature, an artist who was capable of great reliefs, a universally good composer. His work was pure and without embellishments, because he only imitated what was real and concentrated on making his figures stand out. He was as good and able at perspective as anyone else of his time, and painted with great ease. He died very young, at the age of twenty-six.   C. LANDINO
Preamble to: *Comment on the Divine Comedy*, 1481.

The artist Masaccio, a wonderful man, painted in Florence and elsewhere. He died at the approximate age of twenty-seven.
. . . as far as we know, he was considered the finest master who has ever lived.   A. MANETTI
Famous Men of Florence from 1400 onwards.
Last quarter of fifteenth century.

Tommaso Masacci, of Florence, an artist nicknamed Masaccio, was a great imitator of Nature, worked with great ease, gave great relief but no embellishments to his figures. He died in Rome, some say of poison, at the age of twenty-six. He was greatly loved by Filippi di Ser Brunellesche, to whom he taught much. And when Filippo heard of his death he showed great grief. His servants heard him frequently repeat: "We have suffered a great loss."   A. BILLI
Beginning of sixteenth century.

Tommaso of Florence, nicknamed Masaccio, showed by his perfect works, how those who take for their inspiration anything but Nature—mistress of all masters—weary themselves in vain.
LEONARDO DA VINCI
Atlantic Codex,
End of fifteenth or beginning of sixteenth centuries.

Indeed we owe a great debt to those who, by their efforts, showed us the way to the top. With regard to painting we are indebted first of all to Masaccio who first painted people's feet actually standing on the ground, and by so doing eliminated that awkwardness, common to all artists before him, of having the figures standing on tiptoe. We must also be grateful to him for having given his figures such liveliness and relief that he deserves the same credit as if he had invented Art itself. All things painted before him were artificial paintings, whereas his works, compared to those of his rivals and imitators, appear alive and real, rather than counterfeit.   G. VASARI
Lives of the Artists, 1550.

Before Masaccio artists painted without drawing. They knew nothing about perspective, front and rear, composition, harmony, movement of the figures, or natural pleats in clothing. Masaccio must have become suddenly aware of all this, it would seem, because in his paintings one constantly finds the new principles of each of those things, or at least some attempt at establishing them, in addition to the masterly ease, unknown beforehand, with which he handled his brushes.   T. PATCH
Life of Masaccio, 1770.

It is an astonishing thought that in a city rich with talent as was Florence, and in which art was constantly encouraged, no one, even imitating Masaccio, could attain the heights that he had reached without any imitation.   L. LANZI
History of Italian Painting, 1795–6.

As antiquity has left us nothing, in terms of chiaroscuro, of color, of perspective and of expression, Masaccio, rather than the renovator, is to be considered the creator of painting.

STENDHAL
History of Painting in Italy, 1811–17.

45

Born in poverty, almost unknown during the best part of his short life, he carried out singlehanded the greatest revolution ever known in painting.

. . . Masaccio increased the importance of drawing; he freed his figures from those miserable tight garments which appeared to imprison rather than clothe the body. He mastered the foreshortened view and gave to his figures real life and movement, making it impossible for others, after him, to return to the old-fashioned aridity.

E. DELACROIX
Revue de Paris, 1830.

Masaccio proved to be—as no other of his contemporaries, a true follower of the great and strict laws of composition laid down by Giotto. As one glorious period ended he opened a new one: his beautiful and majestic manner, if on the one hand connects him to Giotto, on the other paves the way for Ghirlandaio, Fra' Bartolommeo and Raphael.

G. B. CAVALCASELLE and S. CROWE
History of Painting in Italy, 1864.

Giotto born again, starting where death had cut short his advance, instantly making his own all that had been gained during his absence, and profiting by the new conditions, the new demands—imagine such an avatar, and you will understand Masaccio.

. . . Types, in themselves of the manliest, he presents with a sense of the materially significant which makes us realize to the utmost their power and dignity; and the spiritual significance thus gained he uses to give the highest import to the event he is portraying; this import, in turn, gives a higher value to the types, and thus, whether we devote our attention to his types or to his action, Masaccio keeps us on a high plane of reality and significance.

B. BERENSON
The Italian Painters of the Renaissance, 1896.

Masaccio conquered for painting the world of light: an intense light, strongly contrasting with the shadows, is the means by which he ensures the plasticity of his figures. Not the diffused luminosity, the quasi-radiance of the flesh, nor the vivid colors employed by Masolino, but a light which proceeds from a well-chosen direction and, as in real life, strikes each object in a different way, falling directly upon one, or barely touching another. In such a play of light and shade, color no longer appears to be blended, as in Masolino's pictures, but becomes dull in the clothing, and earthy, tinged with red, in the flesh.

P. TOESCA
Masolino da Panicale, 1908.

Masaccio knew that perspective's main function is to give a more definite feeling of the work's structure. He knew it as a means to set the scene, to support the various groups of figures, to give a clear vision of the many relationships of size and distance. He knew that, ultimately, perspective aims at strengthening the unity of the work and at transmitting to the spectator the feeling of its harmony. That is why, in the paintings most clearly his, we find a symmetry of composition and a balance between the various parts, which are evident not only in the central perspective, but also in the distribution of all masses, in the concentration of figures around the main focal points, and in the harmony of their movements. This science of composition is indeed one of the most outstanding features of Masaccio's art; perhaps this is what puts him into a class of his own among the artists of his time, and raises him far above them all.   J. MESNIL
Masaccio and the Beginning of the Renaissance, 1927.

Chiaroscuro, being so fluid, produces an atmospheric effect which foretells of future developments. It absorbs almost completely the outlines, so that we are aware only of their function of formal definition and of the figure's movement, but not of their presence. This was the result of Masaccio's admirable synthesis, combining linear drawing, chiaroscuro, light and color.

47

In his paintings, while color and light create tonal combinations, color, blending with light and with chiaroscuro, contributes to the creation of form. This was perfectly consistent with the artist's plastic research and with the aims of the Florentine artistic world.

... Masaccio's powerful humanity found a preordained world, proportionate to it, and which it could dominate. This too was consistent with the Florentine tradition from Giotto to Michelangelo.

M. SALMI
Masaccio, 1932.

To express his concept of stoical humanity Masaccio used to the utmost his plastic sense. . . . His plasticity rejects any detailed analysis of anatomy and clothing. His plans become immediately concrete, thanks to the boldest synthesis which does not appear as such only because it is so coherent. And because of this heavy, elementary plasticity, which overcomes all contingencies, the spirit of his images appears as it does, contained and yet impassioned, convinced of Divine omnipotence but still aware of itself; self-assured on earth, as he who is master of his land, but with his eyes turned to the sky, as he who is conscious of being immortal. Architecture, mountains, and plants, undergo this same process of simplification, and become the symbols of architecture, of mountains, of plants; they offer no detail, no concession to decorative complacence: all is sacrificed to the extreme spirituality of the figures.

M. PITTALUGA
Masaccio, 1935.

After his journey through Hell where—there being no light— there can be no shadow, Dante emerged into the southern light of Mount Purgatory, and forthwith was recognized as a mortal by the shadow his body cast on the ground. Perhaps Masaccio meditated on this, perhaps on this basis he decided that space, as conceived by Brunelleschi, could become inhabited, pulsating with life, populated by the new, energetic breed of men such as we meet in his works.

From this certainty, which bursts out as a concept of unlimited action, springs the world painted by Masaccio. Its drama, enacted by men determined to see it through, remains one of the highest testimonials to the human spirit in the history of Italian art.   R. LONGHI
The Carmine Frescos, Masaccio and Dante, 1950.

BIBLIOGRAPHICAL NOTE

The principal sources used for this study of Masaccio are brief records left by writers of the fifteenth and beginning of the sixteenth centuries: Cristoforo Landino, Antonio Manetti, the *Book of Antonio Billi*, as derived from the Strozzi and Petrei Codices and from the *Anonimo Magliabechiano*, and the two editions of Vasari's *Lives* (1550 and 1568). All these records are collected in the special memorial edition published by *Miscellanea d'Arte*, Florence, 1903 (pp.153–96). Masaccio's works are also listed in the oldest guidebook of Florence, compiled by Albertini, called *Memoriale di molte statue et picture sono nella inclyta cipta' di Florentia* (1510).

The many works published on Masaccio before 1929 are listed in an excellent study by Odoardo H. Giglioli, "Masaccio—an essay based on 'reasoned bibliography'", published in the *Bulletin of the Italian Royal Institute of Archaeology and History of Art* (1929, pp. 55–101). Quoted here among the most recent publications are the monographs and most important studies, there being no mention of those dealing only with specialized questions.

J. MESNIL. *Masaccio et les débuts de la Renaissance*, The Hague 1927.

A. SCHMARSOW. *Masolino-Masaccio*, Leipzig 1928.

H. LINDBERG. *On the problem of Masolino and Masaccio*, Stockholm 1931 (containing bibliography).

M. SALMI. *Masaccio*. First edition, Rome 1932; second edition, Milan 1948.

R. OERTEL. *Masaccio Fruhwerke*, Marburg 1933.

P. TOESCA. "Masaccio", in *Enciclopedia Italiana*, vol. XXII, Rome 1934.

M. PITTALUGA. *Masaccio*, Florence 1935 (containing extensive bibliography).

R. LONGHI. "Fatti di Masolino e di Masaccio", in *La Critica d'Arte*, nos. XXV–XXVI, 1940–1.

K. STEINBART. *Masaccio*, Vienna 1947.

U. PROCACCI. "Sulla cronologia delle opere di Masacchio e di Masolino tra il 1425 e il 1428", in *Rivista d'Arte*, vol. XXVIII, 1953 Yearbook.

U. PROCACCI. "Il Vasari e la conservazione degli affreschi della Capella Brancacci al Carmine e della Trinità in Santa Maria Novella", in *Scritti di Storia dell'Arte in onore di Lionello Venturi*, Rome 1956.

For further detailed study, the reader should refer to the second edition of Salmi's monograph, which is to date the most comprehensive work on Masaccio.

REPRODUCTIONS

ACKNOWLEDGEMENT FOR PLATES

Plates 1, 10, 16, 17, 44, 54 and 70: *Alinari*. Plates 5 to 9 and 84: *National Gallery, London*. Plates 14, 26, 40–41, 43, 45, 61, 68–69 and 83: *Anderson*. Plates 15: *Sovrintendenza alle Gallerie, Naples*. Plates 28, 30, 50, 51, 53: *Brogi*. Plate 85: *Gardner Museum, Boston, Mass., U.S.A.*

All the other photographs in black and white are from the *Gabinetto della Fotografico Sovrintendenza alle Gallerie, Florence*.

The selection of photographs for the color plates was entrusted on behalf of the publishers to Claudio Emmer.

MADONNA WITH CHILD, ST ANNE AND ANGELS, Florence, Uffizi
Detail of plate I

Plate I. MADONNA WITH CHILD, ST ANNE AND ANGELS,
Florence, Uffizi

Plate 2. *Detail of plate 1*

Plate 3. *Detail of plate 1*

Plate 4. *Detail of plate 1*

Plate 5. VIRGIN AND CHILD, London, National Gallery

Plate 6. *Detail of plate 5*

Plate 7. *Detail of plate 5*

Plate 8. *Detail of plate 5*

Plate 9. *Detail of plate 5*

Plate 10. ST PAUL, Pisa, Museo Nazionale

Plate 11. ST ANDREW, Vienna, Lanckoronski Collection

Plate 12. SS AUGUSTUS AND JEROME, Berlin, Staatliche Museen

Plate 13. TWO CARMELITE SAINTS, Berlin, Staatliche Museen

Plate 14. CRUCIFIXION, Naples, Gallerie Nazionale di Capodimonte

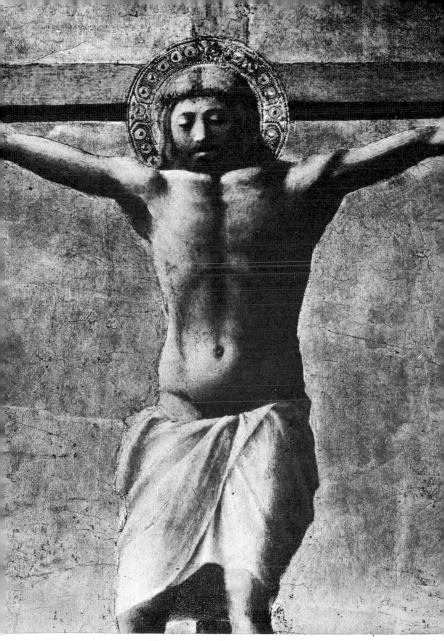

Plate 15. *Detail of plate 14*

Plate 16. *Detail of plate 14*

CRUCIFIXION, Naples, Gallerie Nazionale. *Detail of plate 14*

Plate 17. *Detail of plate 14*

Plate 18. ADORATION OF THE MAGI, Berlin, Staatliche Museen

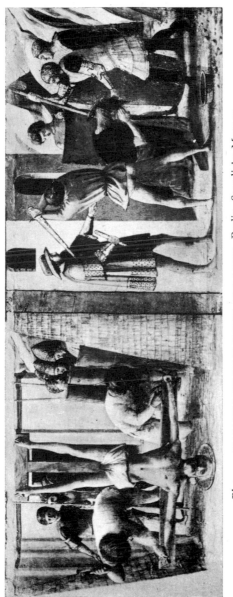

Plate 19. MARTYRDOM OF SS PETER AND JOHN, Berlin, Staatliche Museen

Plate 20. *Detail of plate 18*

Plate 21. *Detail of plate 18*

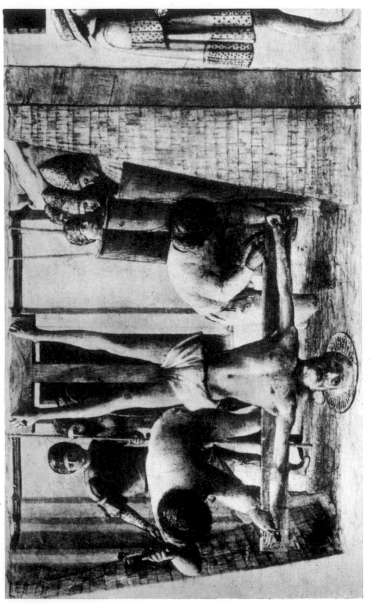

Plate 22. *Detail of plate 19*

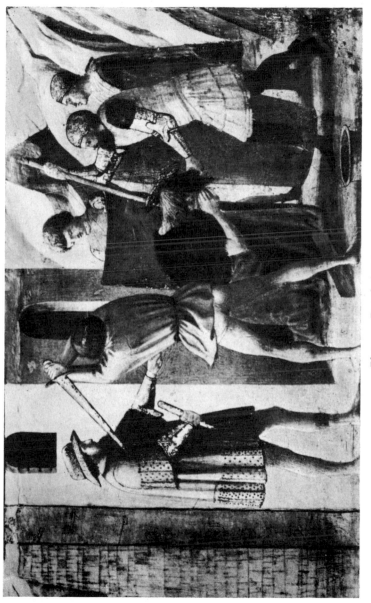

Plate 23. *Detail of plate 19*

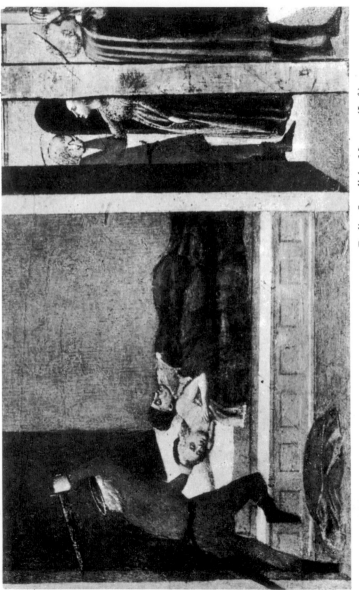

Plate 24. LEGENDS OF SS JULIAN AND NICHOLAS, Berlin, Staatliche Museen (*Left*)

Plate 25. LEGENDS OF SS JULIAN AND NICHOLAS, Berlin, Staatliche Museen (*Right*)

Plate 26. HOLY TRINITY, Florence, Church of Santa Maria Novella

Plate 27. *Detail of plate 26*

Plate 28. *Detail of plate 26*

Plate 29. *Detail of plate 26*

Plate 30. *Detail of plate 26*

Plate 31. *Detail of plate 26*

Plate 32. *Detail of plate 26*

Plate 33. *Detail of plate 26*

Plate 34. BAPTISM OF THE NEOPHYTES, Florence,
Church of the Carmine, Brancacci Chapel

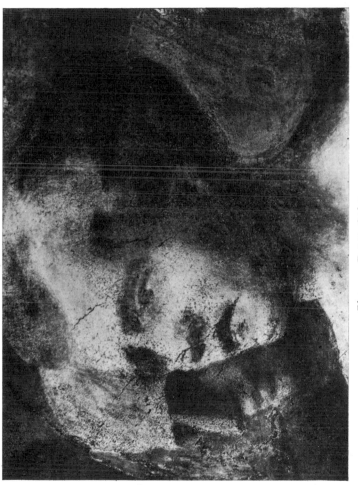

Plate 39. *Detail of plate 34*

Plate 40–41. THE TRIBUTE MÓNEY, Florence, Brancacci Chapel

Plate 42. *Detail of plate 40–41*

Plate 43. *Detail of plate 40–41*

Plate 44. *Detail of plate 40–41*

Plate 45. *Detail of plate 40–41.*

Plate 46. *Detail of plate 40–41*

Plate 47. *Detail of plate 40-41*

Plate 48. *Detail of plate 40–41*

THE TRIBUTE MONEY, Florence, Brancacci Chapel. *Detail of plate 40–41*

Plate 49. *Detail of plate 40–41*

Plate 50. *Detail of plate 40–41*

Plate 51. THE EXPULSION OF ADAM AND EVE,
Florence, Brancacci Chapel

Plate 52. *Detail of plate 51*

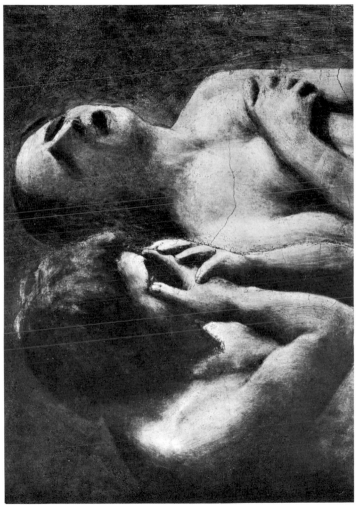

Plate 53. *Detail of plate 51*

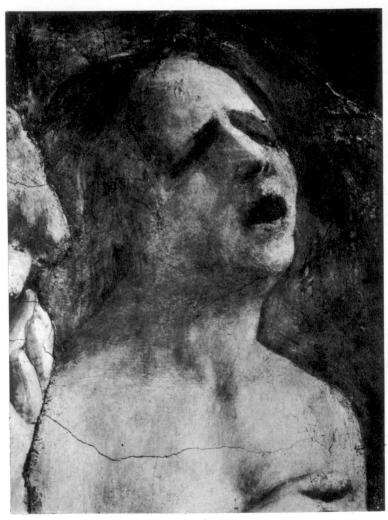

Plate 54. *Detail of plate 51*

Plate 55. ST PETER HEALING THE SICK WITH HIS SHADOW,
Florence, Brancacci Chapel

Plate 56. *Detail of plate 55*

Plate 57. *Detail of plate 55*

Plate 58. *Detail of plate 55*

Plate 59. *Detail of plate 55*

Plate 60. *Detail of plate 55*

Plate 61. ST PETER DISTRIBUTING THE COMMON GOODS, Florence, Brancacci Chapel

Plate 62. *Detail of plate 61*

Plate 63. *Detail of plate 61*

Plate 64. *Detail of plate 61*

ST PETER DISTRIBUTING THE COMMON GOODS, Florence, Brancacci
Chapel. *Detail of plate 61*

Plate 65. *Detail of plate 61*

Plate 66. *Detail of plate 61*

Plate 67. *Detail of plate 61*

Plate 68–69. THE RESURRECTION OF THE SON OF
THE KING OF ANTIOCH AND ST PETER ENTHRONED
Florence, Brancacci Chapel

Plate 70. *Detail of plate 68-69*

Plate 71. *Detail of plate 68–69*

Plate 72. *Detail of plate 68–69*

Plate 73. *Detail of plate 68–69*

Plate 74. *Detail of plate 68–69*

Plate 75. *Detail of plate 68–69*

Plate 76. *Detail of plate 68–69*

Plate 77. *Detail of plate 68–69*

Plate 78. *Detail of plate 68–69*

Plate 79. *Detail of plate 68–69*

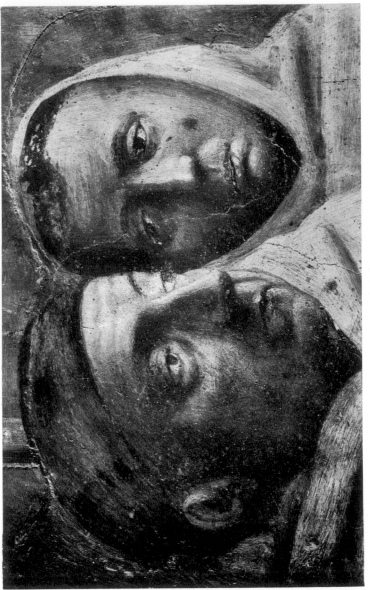

Plate 80. *Detail of plate 68–69*

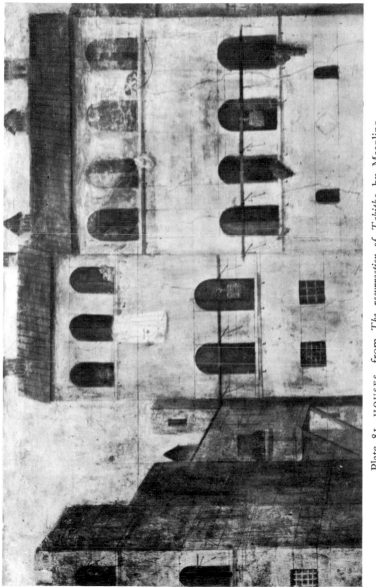

Plate 81. HOUSES, from *The resurrection of Tabitha* by Masolino, Florence, Brancacci Chapel

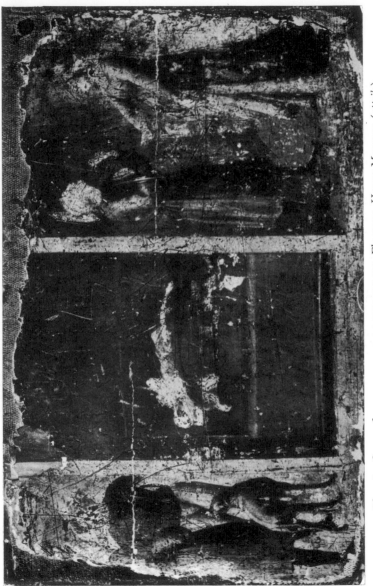

Plate 82. Scenes from THE LIFE OF ST JULIAN, Florence, Horne Museum (*attrib.*)

Plate 83. CRUCIFIXION, Rome, Church of San Clemente (*attrib.*)

Plate 84. SS JEROME AND JOHN THE BAPTIST,
London, National Gallery (*attrib.*)

Plate 85. PORTRAIT OF A GENTLEMAN,
Boston, Gardner Museum (*attrib.*)

Plate 86. MADONNA WITH CHILD, SS JOHN THE BAPTIST AND
MICHAEL, Montemarciano, Church of Madonna delle Grazie (*attrib.*)

Plate 87. MADONNA OF THE UMILTA,
Washington, National Gallery of Art
(*attrib.*)

Plate 88. REPAST FOR A CHILDBIRTH, Berlin, Staatliche Museen
(*attrib.*)